About the Author

I am an iTaukei Fijian mum, raising a family with my loving husband, in the beautiful Aotearoa (New Zealand). Born in my homeland, Fiji, I migrated at the age of twelve to New Zealand with my parents. I remember dreaming of the possibility of an iTaukei girl like myself writing a few words on a page that would inspire children around the world.

A teenager's dream has now become a reality in motherhood. I am humbled and excited to share this piece of literature with every parent who believes in raising great thinkers. I have been blessed to be introduced to the world of appreciation, learning, exploration, discovery, and excitement since having my babies. My writing is influenced by my daily experiences as a mum and wife and I wish for it to be a guide to every children's development and thinking.

I thank God for this wonderful experience to reveal a piece of my heart with you.

Jake's I'm Sorry Letters

Mele Bukateci-Drivationo

Jake's I'm Sorry Letters

Nightingale Books

NIGHTINGALE PAPERBACK

A CIP catalogue record for this title is
available from the British Library.
ISBN 9781838750978

Nightingale Books is an imprint of
Pegasus Elliot MacKenzie Publishers Ltd.
www.pegasuspublishers.com

First Published in 2021

Nightingale Books
Sheraton House Castle Park
Cambridge England

Printed & Bound in Great Britain

Dedication

To my Heavenly Father – thank you for the gift.

All my praises to you.

My loving husband Jone, my great thinker, Samuel and my great explorer, Noya – thank you for believing in mummy. I love you twice, always and forever.

To my parents, Taniela & Nora, and siblings, Tu Varani, Ria, Mana and to my Talailai – thank you for keeping me grounded with your steady love.

To our Tatu & Nau – your continuous prayers is a true example of perseverance.

To my extended family, thank you for the fabric of love and knowledge you wove within me.

My nephews, nieces, and little cousins- keep reaching for your greatness and have God lead your journey.

Boom! A rock hit Beth, the hippo's, head.

"Ouch!" She looked up and saw Jake, the monkey, laughing out LOUD!

"Hehe!" Jake beamed as he swung on the next vine.

He tricked Beth again.

Splash! Water poured all over Paul, the parrot, when he tugged on the fruitlike water-balloon. "Squawk!" he cried, as he shook of the water to dry himself.

Jake had tied the water balloon next to Paul's branch.

"Tricked yah!" he laughed. "I'm a great trickster," Jake said pointing at the water-balloon.

But not everyone in the jungle thought so.

They were unhappy with Jake. He always played tricks and no one wanted to be his friend. All the jungle animals, including Beth and Paul gathered to talk about not inviting Jake to the upcoming jungle party. Everyone agreed.

"Yes, we should not invite Jake because he will just ruin everything," said Noya, the bear.

All the jungle animals were busy talking, and no one realised that Jake was hanging from a nearby tree.

He was sad. He had heard everything.

Jake didn't realise he had made all the jungle animals unhappy. He wanted to go to the jungle party too.

I AM SORRY
I AM SORRY

Jake swung home that evening with a heavy heart.

'How do I say sorry to all the animals?' he thought to himself.

His eyes searched his tree as he sat on the short branch with the brown vine. Then it came to him! He will write everyone an 'I'm Sorry Letter'.

He started writing away and waited for the afternoon.

Jake was going to deliver his 'I'm Sorry Letters' when all the jungle animals were home.

I AM SORRY
I AM SORRY

Jake placed a pink 'I'm Sorry Letter' on the black rock outside Noya's cave.

I AM
SORRY

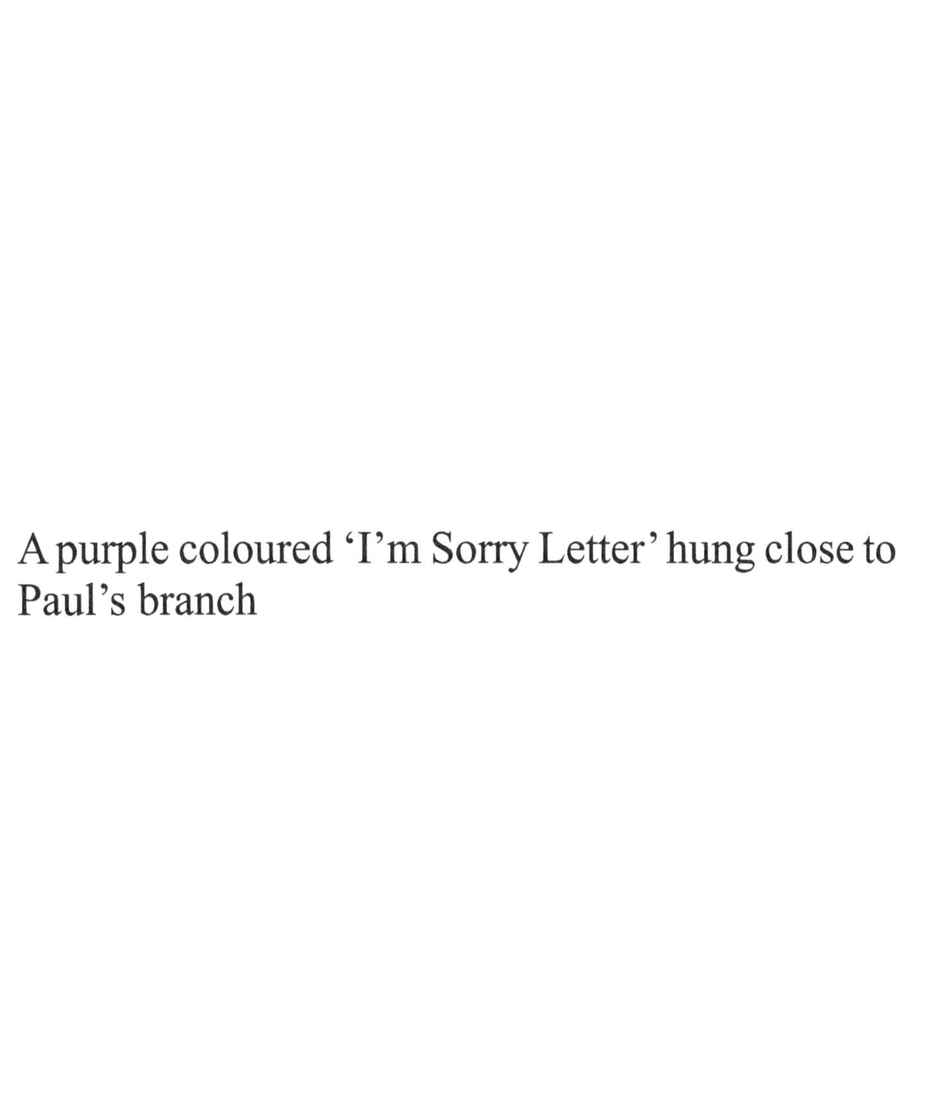

A purple coloured 'I'm Sorry Letter' hung close to Paul's branch

I AM
SORRY

He had also written a blue 'I'm Sorry Letter' for Beth, the hippo.

I AM
SORRY

A green 'I'm Sorry Letter' for Ori, the rhino.

I AM SORRY

A yellow 'I'm Sorry Letter' for Judah, the lion.

I AM
SORRY

A red 'I'm Sorry Letter" for Samuel, the tiger.

I AM
SORRY

And a bright orange 'I'm Sorry Letter' for Joy, the flamingo.

Jake felt pleased. He did not want to make his friends sad anymore.

I AM SORRY
I AM SORRY
I AM SORRY
I AM SORRY
I AM SORRY
I AM SORRY

The next morning, Noya, Paul, Beth, Ori, Samuel and Joy gathered by the Waterfall and showed each other their 'I'm Sorry Letters'.

"Did you get a letter too?" asked Noya as Judah joined them.

"Yes, a yellow one," he said sighing heavily.

They had felt disappointed in themselves for not including Jake in their jungle party.

They knew they were wrong and wanted to make it up to him.

Meanwhile, Jake woke up and wondered how everyone felt about his 'I'm Sorry Letters'.

'I hope they can forgive me,' he thought to himself, as he swung towards his favourite tree. When he came close, he saw a big black bag hanging from one of the branches.

'I wonder what this is?' he thought to himself as he started tugging it open.

I AM
SORRY

Riiiiiiippp! The zip gave way and different coloured balloons flew up into the branches. Pink ones, purple ones, yellow ones and all the colours you can imagine!

"SURPRISE!" A chorus rang out!

Jake jumped!

He looked around and saw all the jungle animals smiling at him. They had startled him! Jake laughed! He was so happy to see all his friends. He was starting to miss playing with them.

"Come to our jungle party, Jake!" Samuel, the tiger cheered with all the animals joining in too.

The next day, all the jungle animals and Jake had the best jungle party ever! No tricks this time!

9 781838 750978